MY DOCTOR BOOK

THE NOT-SO-SCARY ADVENTURES OF BROTHERS: ANDERSON & RILEY.

written by

Dr. Tiffany Otto Knipe

illustrations by

Martha Napier

Archway Publishing books may be ordered through booksellers or by contacting:

Archway Publishing
1663 Liberty Drive
Bloomington, IN 47403
www.archwaypublishing.com
1 (888) 242-5904

Because of the dynamic nature of the Internet, any web addresses or links contained in this book may have changed since publication and may no longer be valid. The views expressed in this work are solely those of the author and do not necessarily reflect the views of the publisher, and the publisher hereby disclaims any responsibility for them.

Any people depicted in stock imagery provided by Thinkstock are models, and such images are being used for illustrative purposes only.
Certain stock imagery © Thinkstock.

Graphics: Martha Napier

ISBN: 978-1-4808-2960-2 (sc)
ISBN: 978-1-4808-2961-9 (hc)
ISBN: 978-1-4808-2959-6 (e)

Print information available on the last page.

Archway Publishing rev. date: 5/12/2016

ARCHWAY PUBLISHING

To My Boys –
who inspire me with their endless curiosity and delight.

My name is Anderson, and I'm six years old.
My little brother Riley is home today with bad sniffles and a cold.

He's got fever and sneezes coughing and wheezes,
rashes and itches, and maybe needs stitches!

We're off to the doc says our mother – but not without protest from my
little brother. "I'm scared, and I'm mad, and i don't want to go!"
Riley, I said, the doctor's quite nice. If you have an ill, she'll give you a pill;

RX
RILEY
TAKE
ONE 2

M T W T F S S
Rest ——→
Rest ——→
Play!

or a bandaid instead or maybe some ice for the aches and the scrapes.
If your throat is sore, congestion's in your chest,
she'll prescribe some medicine or just a few days rest.

She'll know what to do she's a PEDIATRICAN after all
taking care of kids big ones and small!

She will help you feel better really, there's no need to bawl!

She has a STETHOSCOPE to listen to the heart's rhythms and beats.

And also a THERMOMETER to measure a body's extra heat.

And to check your ears she has an OTOSCOPE it's like
a fancy flashlight!

Then she'll check how big you are by measuring your weight and height!

There's also lots of sparkly band-aids for the boo-boos and the bruises.
These are just some of the doctor tools she uses!

She's got her own kids too, and works next door
so let's go see her office for a Pediatric Tour!

161

161
Hudson

So we quietly tiptoed to her office next door and peered through
the window for our Doctor-Adventure-Explore!

Doc washed her hands with sudsy soap and water.
Then in came her patient - a worried mommy and her daughter.

Doc asked them questions like what hurts and where?
Her voice was kind and she had a smile so friendly
the little girl relaxed then pointed to her belly.
I think Doc also used a tiny pinch of magic - because in a flash
the girl's fear was gone, and POOF — away went all her panic!

Doc put the stethoscope gently on the girl's chest.
I saw her listen carefully to her heartbeats and her breaths.

Doc gently lay her hands right on the little girls tummy.

"OOOCH that's where it hurts! I'm feeling rather crummy."

Then Doc said: "AHA! You need this medicine to drink
It tastes quite good and guess what...it's PINK!

It will make you feel much better in just a day or two.
And in no time at all you will be eating ice-cream and
playing peek-a-boo!"

Our Pediatrician has a super-fun career - she's like a MAGICIAN...

making the fears and ouches disappear!

Then Doc walked into the next room and waiting for her there,
was a mommy and a daddy and a baby with no hair!
They said he was a newborn — only three days old.
And now our Doc has a whole new role.

The baby was crying and the parents asked:
"What to do?" Doc said: "Give a bottle and a hug, then check
his diaper for some poo." The baby stopped his sobbing
and the parents said: "THANK YOU!"

On to the next room - a boy to get measured and weighed.
Doc told him how to stay healthy and keep the COOTIES away!

"If you eat your broccoli and finish your peas
and drink lots of milk you won't cough or sneeze!
You will grow BIG and stay very strong
then you wont need to come here all the year long."

AAHHH
AAAHHHHH
AAAAHHHHHHHHHHHH
AAAAHHHHHHHHHHH
AAAAHHHHHHH

"Open your mouth, please and wiggle your toes
then bend your knees and let me look up your nose.

Now stick out your tongue as far as it goes ...
AAAAAAAAHHHHHHHHHHHHHHHHHHHHHHHHHHHHH"

D
IS
FOR
DINOSAUR

Doc examined him from his toes to his top. She said:
"To keep you healthy and strong,
I need to give you a shot.

I know it seems scary but this super-fast prick will help you stay well
so you will not get sick!" She gave him the shot and he barely flinched!
The anticipation was much worse than the actual pinch!

He left the office smiling with nothing to fear.

"Thank you, Doctor! I will see you again next year."

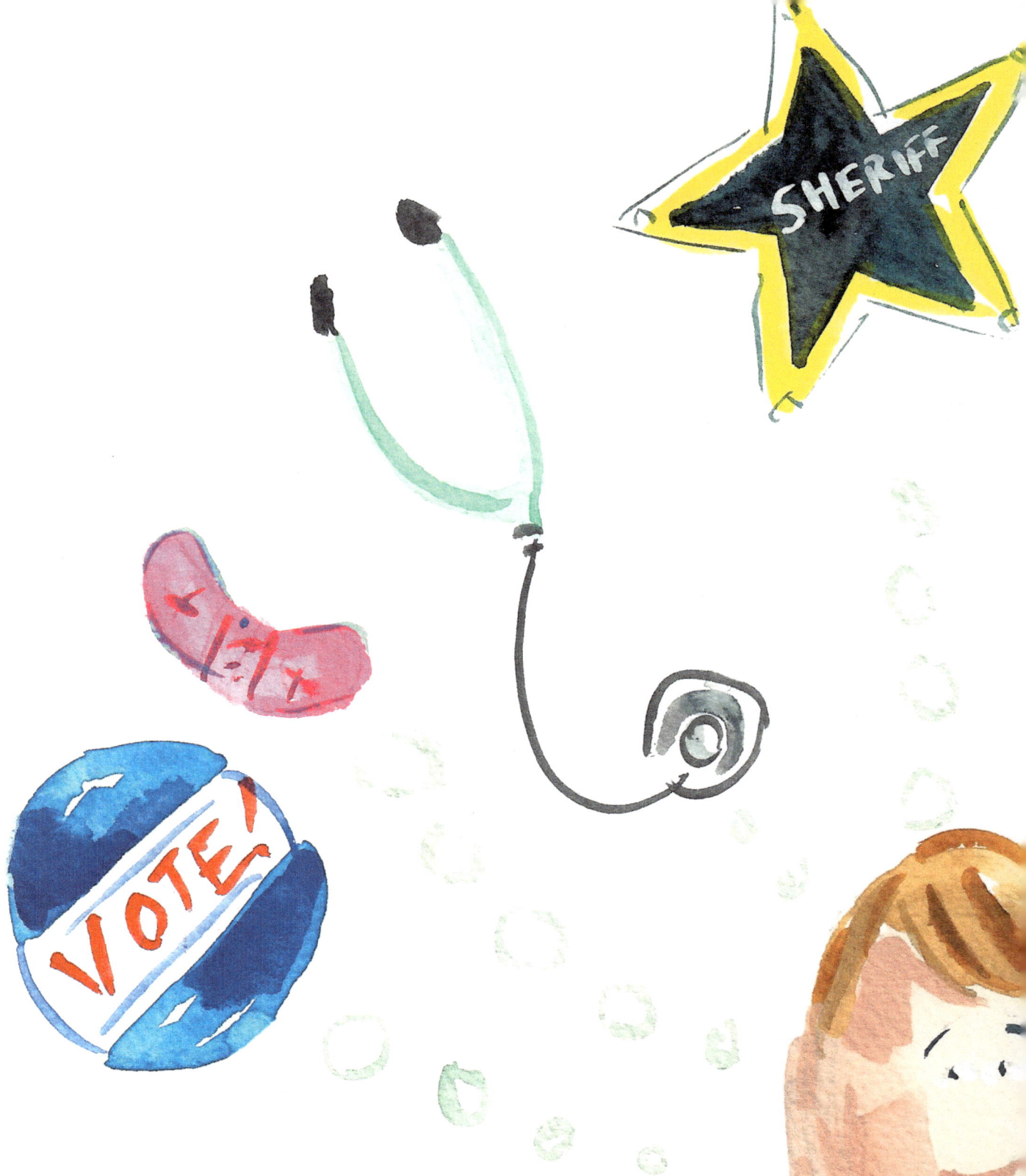

Time to head back home, there was a lot that
we had seen. I want to be a doctor
I have a brand new dream

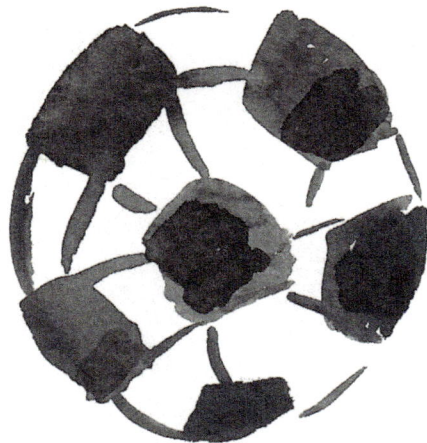

Or... maybe a fireman   Policeman
Soccer star   Or politician ...
Or maybe like our Doc, a PEDIATRICIAN !

On our way out the door my brother and I paused for one last question
we wanted to understand MORE about this doctor profession.

"What's it like to be a Doctor, Doc?" My brother and I asked.

"The job is tough, the responsibility is vast. But there is nothing better than to have fun while you work.
It is something unique, a really great perk.

Do what you LOVE and love what you do,
but no matter what, boys— just always be YOU!"

Then with our Doctor's kind aid Riley's COUGH and SNEEZE
at last began to fade. And his temp
returned to a normal ninety-eight degrees!

"Thanks, Doc," we said! "We learned so much today "
Then we saw the sun overhead
and ran to the park to skip, jump and play.

THE END.

GET TO KNOW
MY DOCTOR

{next time you see your doc, get to know them better
by asking the below questions}

Your Doctor's Name: _____

Their Favorite Color: _____

Favorite Healthy Snack: _____

What did you want to: _____
be when you grew up?

What's your favorite thing: _____
about being a pediatrician?

{draw a picture in the frame of your dog}

MEET THE

Dr. Tiffany Otto Knipe, MD, FAAP

Washington Market Pediatrics, New York

DOCTOR

Dr. Tiffany is the founding pediatrician of TriBeCa, Manhattan's premiere boutique pediatric office, Washington Market Pediatrics. Dr. Tiffany is a board-certified pediatrician and a specialist in Pediatric Infectious Diseases. She completed her undergraduate training at University of Pennsylvania, then went on to medical school at Jefferson Medical College. She completed residency at New York Presbyterian – Weill Cornell Medical Center and then completed three additional years of fellowship training in Pediatric Infectious Diseases at Yale University and New York University Langone Medical Center.

Dr. Tiffany currently serves as a Clinical Instructor at New York Presbyterian – Weill Cornell Medical Center and New York University Langone Medical Center. She is also the pediatric expert for the new on-line platform, Motherly (http://www.mother.ly) which guides women on a personalized, week-by-week journey to motherhood.

Dr. Tiffany and her husband are long-time residents of TriBeCa and love raising their two young boys in the neighborhood {fun fact: Dr. Tiffany was inspired by her own boys to create the dynamic brother duo, Anderson and Riley}. As fixtures in the New York community, Dr. Tiffany and her family are often out playing sports at Pier 25, picnicking in Battery Park and planting in their garden in Washington Market Park.

MEET THE

Martha Napier, Illustrator & Designer

Marnani Design Studio, LLC {www.marnani.com}

ARTIST

Martha Napier is the creative force behind the whimsical illustration brand, Marnani Design. Formerly a Lead Womens Designer at Michael Kors, Martha uses a keen sense of fashion in all of her illustrations. Martha has illustrated for the the likes of Neiman Marcus, Barneys New York, Gap Brands, The New Yorker, and her work has graced the pages of the New York Times, The New York Post, Better Homes and Gardens, and Luxury Magazine, among others. In 2015, Martha was named a top illustrator to follow by InStyle Magazine.

Martha is especially known for her live illustration services for high end events, and during New York Fashion Week {with nods from the likes of fashion elite, Bill Cunningham of the New York Times, Suzy Menkes of Vogue, and Linda Fargo of Bergdorf Goodman}.

Martha's eponymous illustration business, Marnani Design, offers a watercolor themed paper suite, small housewares, apparel and accessories, and custom family and pet portraits. Her work is always in celebration of color, whimsy & joy.

You can see more of Martha's whimsical work on her site, www.marnani.com.

Martha is especially thrilled to help bring Anderson and Riley to life in watercolor, as she is an expectant mother of a baby girl, due in 2016.

CPSIA information can be obtained
at www.ICGtesting.com
Printed in the USA
BVOW07s2303270516

449873BV00012B/48/P